PIANO • VOCAL • GUITAR

MIKA
THE BOY WHO KNEW TOO MUCH

Illustration and Design by DaWack/Mika/Richard Hogg.

ISBN 978-1-4234-9014-2

HAL•LEONARD®
CORPORATION

7777 W. BLUEMOUND RD. P.O. BOX 13819 MILWAUKEE, WI 53213

In Australia Contact:
Hal Leonard Australia Pty. Ltd.
4 Lentara Court
Cheltenham, Victoria, 3192 Australia
Email: ausadmin@halleonard.com.au

Visit Hal Leonard Online at
www.halleonard.com

WE ARE GOLDEN

Words and Music by
MIKA

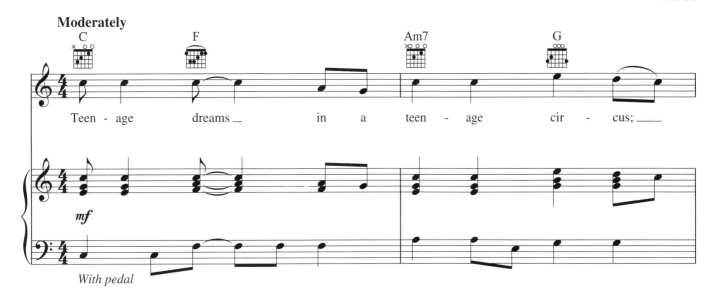

Teen-age dreams ___ in a teen-age cir-cus; ___

run-ning a-round ___ like a clown ___ on pur-pose. Who gives a damn ___ a-bout the

fam-'ly you come from? No giv-ing up ___ when you're young and you want some.

RAIN

Words and Music by MIKA
and JODI MARR

DR. JOHN

Words and Music by
MIKA

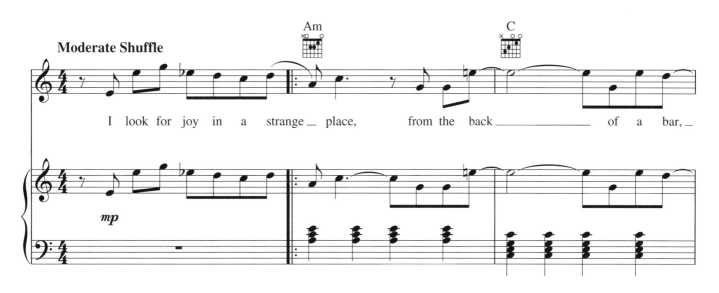

I look for joy in a strange __ place, from the back _____ of a bar, __

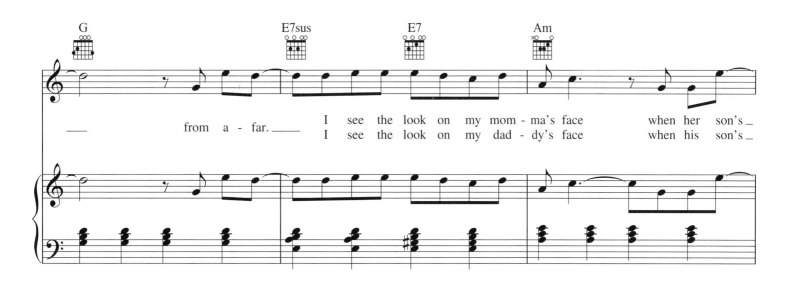

__ from a - far. __ I see the look on my mom - ma's face when her son's __
I see the look on my dad - dy's face when his son's __

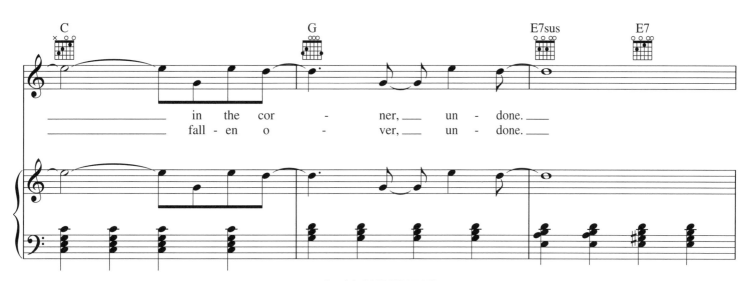

__ in the cor - ner, __ un - done. __
fall - en o - ver, __ un - done. __

I SEE YOU

Words and Music by MIKA
and WALTER AFANASIEFF

BLUE EYES

Words and Music by
MIKA

Your heart is bro - ken,   to
Your heart got bro - ken   on the

Recorded a half step lower.

GOOD GONE GIRL

Words and Music by MIKA
and JODI MARR

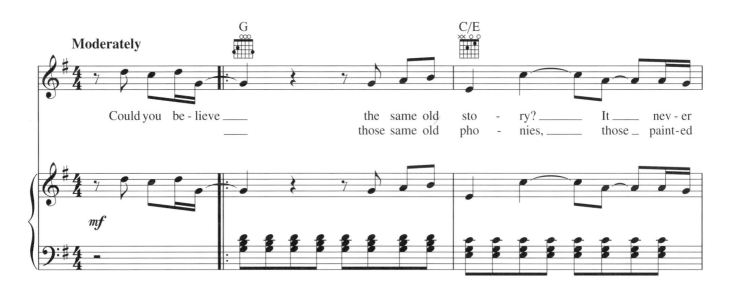

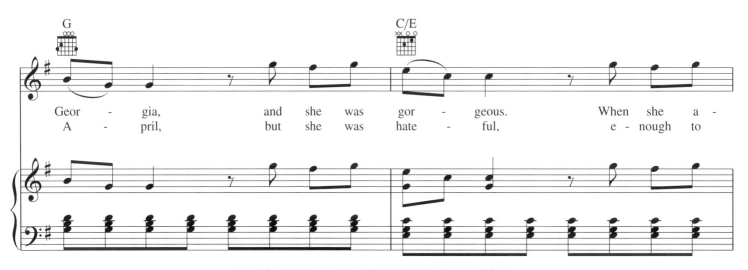

TOUCHES YOU

Words and Music by
MIKA

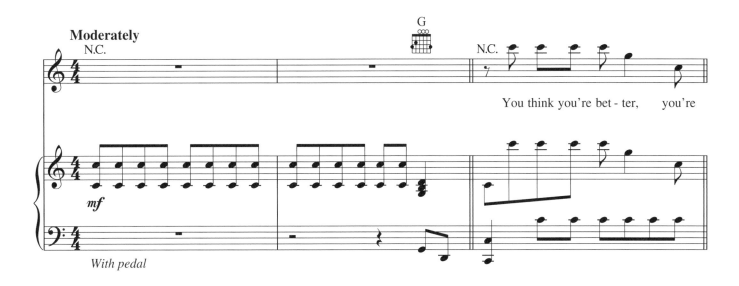

BY THE TIME

Words and Music by MIKA
and IMOGEN HEAP

Moderately slow

(Don't wake up, won't wake up, can't wake up, no, don't wake me up.

Don't wake up, won't wake up, can't wake up, no, don't wake me up.)

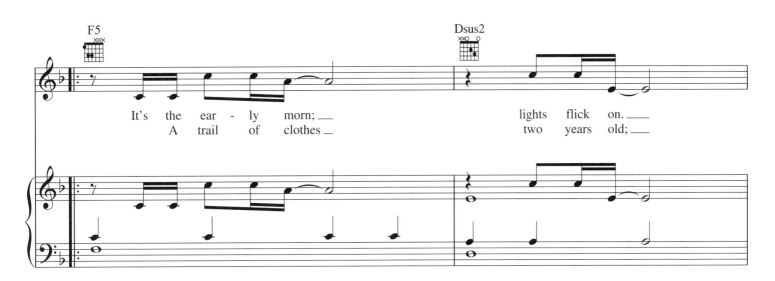

It's the ear-ly morn; ___ lights flick on. ___
A trail of clothes ___ two years old; ___

ONE FOOT BOY

Words and Music by MIKA
and ROB DAVIES

Moderately

What's the mat-ter with go-ing plac-es?
own. Say you like me, not with chang-es?

Take that gross look
Shut up and for-get it!

off your fac-es!
These are my fac-es.

Emp-ty lov-ing makes me sea-sick.
All these col-ors that sur-round me,

What you here for?
all these plac-es

I don't need it.
on-ly drown me.

Lead Vocal 1: I'll say

TOY BOY

Words and Music by MIKA
and JODI MARR

PICK UP OFF THE FLOOR

Words and Music by
MIKA